DEFEATING

THE

ANTICHRIST

WITH

HADITH

BY GREGORY HEARY

The antichrist is an infamous human who will appear near the end of time, gain many religious devotees and persecute true monotheists. It is confirmed the authentic Christ will return from paradise to kill him, however that will be after a time of great turmoil. During the troublesome reign of the antichrist people will need to defend themselves physically but more importantly spiritually from the theological heresies spread by the antichrist. The mission of the antichrist is to get people to disbelieve in the pure monotheism taught by the prophets such as Noah, Abraham, Moses, Jesus and Muhammad and that is how the antichrist defeats his opponents. Defeat is individualistic pertaining to every special soul. Every soul that encounters the message of the antichrist will need to battle it and not all exposed to such battle will win. Some people will be led to hellfire by the antichrist prior to the return of Jesus and other individuals will maintain pure monotheism and this is defeating the antichrist. Victory in this life in this era and every era is to die the death of a believing monotheist. Whereas the only way to prepare and acquire the knowledge necessary to ensure the safety of oneself and one's family is through authentic prophetic teachings available to us in hadith. Many think the battle against the antichrist is to be postponed until his emergence but this notion is entirely incorrect. The only way the generation of monotheists who experience the antichrist will survive is if the previous generations have passed on the important information from the prophets to them. Without prophetic tools that generation will be annihilated by the antichrist. By us publicizing and passing on that information to them we are actively waging war against the antichrist and his future followers essentially equipping the army of Christ with the weapons they need to attain victory. For victory is not merely political via territory but also spiritual, mental and in terms of lifestyle. For you can be defeated by the devil's ally the antichrist before he even emerges or you can be victorious against both enemies and gain reward for fighting against the antichrist by training the next generation to train the next generation all the way until near the end of time thereby getting multiples of rewards for having started a chain reaction of goodness. Therefore teaching about and exposing the falsehood of the antichrist is an act of military warfare and is the best means of fighting the antichrist prior to his emergence. By reading this book and having the intention to equip oneself for the upcoming battle and teach/recruit others by sharing the prophetic data for the future battles should they not occur in your lifetime is to be an active participant in the war against the antichrist. The war is already ongoing! You need not wait for the antichrist to emerge to fight against him, nor does the leader of heresy and falsehood have to emerge to defeat you or infect you or your family, friends and community with heresy and falsehood. The allies of the devil and the allies of our Creator are already at war theologically, spiritually, economically, politically and in some places even militarily. So don't think you are not in a spiritual warzone just because the antichrist isn't personally going house to house yet. If you think you are safe then sadly you've already lost and need to be healed in a major way before it's too late.

An abundance of false information exists about the antichrist as well, because as part of the devilish plot misinformation is just as deadly as absolute falsehood for it is just another shade of ignorance. How better for the devil to combat the prophetic teachings than by inserting false teachings about himself, his allies, the prophets, God and the apocalypse? Therefore it is with dismay that many don't even recognize the prophethood of Muhammad because of such misinformation. Christians have even been misled into thinking he is the antichrist because of false Crusader era propaganda despite the fact that Jesus will kill the antichrist and Jesus did not kill Muhammad. That alone is enough to refute the lie that Muhammad was the antichrist, let alone when the true believer in Christ examines the teachings of Muhammad they will realize him to be the promised prophet of God to correct the corruptions of Christians that occurred after the ascension of Jesus son of Mary into paradise.

The fact of Muhammad peace be upon him being the final Messenger of God is surprising to many Jews and Christians and often considered as heresy as their clerical orders like to lie about Islam and the prophet that was sent by God to correct the lies of religious leaders who Jews and Christians descend from. This book topic doesn't allow elaborate presentation of his proof for prophethood but the evidence is abundant elsewhere for those who have been misinformed. I used to be such a Christian who held anti-Islamic, anti-Muslim pro-Crusader attitudes and the hardest part is not finding the evidence that Muhammad is God's Messenger after

Jesus, but the hard part is overcoming one's own arrogance in thinking you know better prior to research. Most Jews and Christians feel chosen and special and don't think its possible to be wrong or else they'd feel differently than they do so they never ever research. Generations of brainwashing causes this placebo mentality to some extent but the crux is pure arrogance. The problem is Jews and Christians have no actual Scholars amongst them and they place charismatic personalities as their leaders who delude themselves and others with interpretations of corrupted faulty texts that were mistranslated before they were ever penned by heretics and then they have no scholastic transmission of those heretical texts they label as scripture and no prophetic approval or prophetic interpretation. For example if you ask a Jew what Moses said about a verse in their book they don't have a answer from Moses though they falsely claim he is responsible for their Hebrew book despite Moses and David dying before the Hebrew language even existed. Christians are even worse in that they know Jesus didn't write their Greek books and that his disciples didn't know Greek and they know Jesus didn't comment on the texts they have. Thus both Jews and Christians are left to their own satanic opinions which they draw from satanic documents they are told are inspired to admitted non-prophets from God and they never research the Quran to see the difference between genuine speech of God given to a prophet versus what they have because their leaders and devils tell them to be scared to read it. They sincerely think they are specially chosen by God and even have part of God in them via the Holy Ghost and their communion ritual but they are terrified to read the only book in the world that claims to be from God and has been documented as the most popular and widely memorized book of all time; the Quran. It is criminally unjust and arrogant and those who continue to refuse will suffer as a result of such a cowardly bigotry. Truly they admit they have no scriptural analysis from any prophet so that admission is proof enough another prophet must be sent with a new scripture and scriptural analysis so nobody is misled by false preachers. Yet to break down that arrogant placebo barrier of cultish mistrust of anything outside their current co-religionist propaganda can only be done by the Creator of their mind and heart should God wish goodness for them. I digress, as it pertains to the Anti-Christ he is only mentioned indirectly in the

Quran because he was mentioned more directly in the prophetic speech of Muhammad and the Quran is Allah's speech. Both the Hadith and the Quran are revelation but there are differences between them. For those unfamiliar with what a Hadith is, it comprises a statement, action or approval/forbiddance of the prophet Muhammad. Basically the Quran is a book from Allah and the Hadith contains everything that Muhammad taught aside from the Quran. We need the Hadith to explain the Quran correctly according to prophetic understanding. Yet since the era of the prophet ended so long ago how do we know the Hadith we quote is actually from the prophet? This can be verified with what is called the science of hadith.

A hadith's Isnad or chain of narrators may be like this: "***Person E heard from Person D who heard from Person C who was told by Person B that Person A said***: *When I was eating dinner with the prophet pbuh, after he had finished eating a piece of gourd he had selected with his right hand, of which gourd was his favorite food, I saw Muhammad pbuh smile so much his molar teeth were visible and heard him say:*" _____ ". This chain of narrators is called the isnad. Imaam Bukhari said regarding the isnad: ***"The isnad is part of the religion: had it not been for*** *the isnad, whoever wished to would have said whatever he liked.*" While Imam Ash-Shafi'i said in regards to the isnad: "*Whoever attempts to seek and learn hadith without an isnad he is like one who gathers wood at night in the darkness. He picks up wood, not knowing there is a serpant inside.*" Now the Jewish and Christian books do not have any isnads at all, not for even 1 biblical verse. So the isnad is a special proof of authentic information Islam has, which all other faiths and texts of other religions do not have. No other religion can prove that the information they teach today attributing it to X person is the exact same material that was actually taught by X person in the past many years ago. Others faiths say to "trust in God and their texts", Muslims trust in God but prove their religious texts are trustworthy. You trust the material that's from God or his prophets only after it's been proven to really come from God or his prophets. If it's not proven you can't treat it as though it's prophetic, even if it is, because the prophets taught us to follow only what was proven to have truly come from God and forbid monotheists from the blind-following of non-prophets.

There is a methodology for authentication and it is historically scientific. Because of the intellectual honesty of Muslim scholars, the hadiths have various classifications. Islamic scholars admit that not everything people say about Muhammad pbuh is true. There are hadiths which have been forged and fabricated, or are doubtful. Muslim scholars have preserved them, as well as those which are true. There are even books by Muslim scholars devoted to lies people said about Muhammad pbuh detailing who started the lie and why it is a lie. There are also books by Muslim scholars who say: it appears this hadith is true and seems like something Muhammad pbuh would do but we cannot prove it. Then there are classes of hadith which have been proven to be 100% true. No other religion has such intellectual honesty where they say what's true and what's false and what can't be verified; every other religion just says, *"everything we're telling you is true, just trust us"*. A Muslim scholar will tell you if what he is saying has not been proven as well as how strong a religious opinion is. Even non-Muslim scholars have said that Muslims should be proud of their hadith tradition because it is beyond scholastic comparison and no other religion has anything comparable to it. A legal or religious ruling can only be based upon authentic information. Weak(da'eef) or doubtful hadiths by themselves cannot be used to justify doing or not doing something. For a hadith to be classified as sahih or authentic it has to meet a high level of criteria. Usually there must be two separate chains of narration confirming the same tradition. Meaning there must have been more than one witness to the event in question unless it were something specific, such as something that only his wife could witness, but then that has to be mentioned if there is only one chain. The chain must be entirely reliable throughout, meaning all the narrators must have been able to have actually learned from each other and been in the same place at the same time in their lives. Sometimes you will find that person E will say they heard from person D but person D died before person E was born, so it would have been impossible for person E to have learned from person D, or perhaps persons D and E while both alive at the same time and in the same city they may never have actually been able to communicate with each other and share information, these details must be made known and those types of things affect the grade of a hadith. Those in the chain of narration and the scholars must know the biographies of every single person in the chain of each narration, knowing what they did with their life, who they learned from and who they taught, what their morals were like, if they were honest or forgetful and must make sure they are all of reputable character. You cannot just accept a narration at face value, you have to know exactly who these narrators actually were and what they and their memories were like. You cannot just say "I heard from so and so who heard from so and so", when discussing something the prophet Muhammad pbuh said or did, you have to know if "so and so #1" is trustworthy and reliable and you have to know if "so and so #2" is trustworthy and reliable and so on and so forth for the whole chain of narrators for each and every hadith. This is a serious scientific intellectual processing method which is actually inconvenient, however it's the only way to be certain that information is authentic. The authentically proven sound hadith are scholastically more reliable than the bible. The science of hadith is so precise that it even requires critical thinking talents just to contemplate and it overwhelmed me when I first learned about it. I felt like a total fool when I first learned about hadith and realized I could not really prove most of what I thought I knew and considered true. May Allah help us to have correct comprehension, give us understanding, guide us to the truth and make us of those who accept and follow it.

Different scholars have slightly different criteria for grading hadith but some basic principles are:

1. The chain of narration, from Muhammad to the final narrator, must be connected in such a way that every single person in the chain has himself heard or received this narration from the person he is narrating from.

2. All the narrators in the chain must be upright, meaning that they must be:

   a) Muslim

   b) Of the age of puberty

   c) Sane

   d) Not an open sinner

   e) Free from bad habits

3. All the narrators must possess the ability to preserve the hadith precisely letter for letter.

4. The hadith should not contradict other hadiths which have come from more reliable narrators.

5. There are no other hidden weaknesses in the hadith or isnad – such as a hidden gap in the chain of narration.

Upon the absence of any one of the above 5 conditions, the hadith immediately is classed as Weak (da'if). But if all of the conditions are met with the third (preservation) being of a lower degree, then it is classed as Sound/Good (hasan). A hadith is classed as rigorously verified to be 100% true and Authentic (sahih) if it meets the previous 5 conditions and has a high degree of preservation.

In regards to Imam Bukhari's criteria for a hadith he was one of many who strictly would refuse to accept something as being authentic unless he knew of 2 separate isnads for a hadith. So his criteria was even stricter than they needed to be. Basically he required 2 authentic hadiths before he'd consider what either one of them taught as being true. However Imam Bukhari lived a few generations after Muhammad pbuh, were Muslims always so strict about verifying whether something someone said about Muhammad pbuh was true or false? The answer to this is evident in the incident which occurred between Abu Musa Al-Ash'ari and Umar bin Khattab. The background context of this incident is important, this took place only a few years after the death of Muhammad pbuh. At most within 13 years of his death because Umar was the Khalifh at the time this took place. Umar became Khalifh 2 years after Muhammad pbuh died and ruled for 10 years, before dying about 13 years after Muhammad pbuh died. The incident was reported by Abu Musa Al-Ash'ari himself who says what in english means:

"I sought permission to see Umar and I did not have permission after three times. Hence, I left. He called me and said: 'Abdullah, have you found it hard to wait at my door? You better know that people may find it hard to wait at your door.' I said: 'No. I have sought permission three times and I did not obtain it; so I returned, as we have been ordered to do so.' **He said: 'Whom have you heard this from?' I said: 'From the Prophet.' He then said to me: 'Have you heard from the Prophet what we have not heard? You will either support your statement with further evidence or I will certainly punish you.'** *I left him and went to the masjid where I found a member of the Ansar.* <u>I asked them about the case, and they said: 'Is this to be doubted?' I told them what Umar said to me.</u> *They said: 'Then the best way is that the youngest among us should go with you as witness.' Thus, Abu Saeed al-Khudri came with me to Umar and told him: 'We accompanied the Prophet when he went to Saad ibn Ubadah. When he arrived, he offered*

the greeting of peace, 'Assalam alaikum', but no permission was given to him. He repeated his greeting a second time and a third, but no permission was given. He then said: 'We have done what we can.' Then he left. Saad came fast after him, and said: 'Messenger of God! By Him who has sent you with the message of the truth, every time you said the greeting I heard it and replied. But I only wanted that you offer more greetings to me and to my household.' **_Abu Musa then said (to Umar): 'By God I am worthy of trust_** *when it comes to reporting the Prophet's Hadith.'* **_Umar said: 'Certainly. I only wanted to ascertain the matter.'"_**

This incident occurred between the companions of Muhammad pbuh shortly after he had died. None of them ever lied about Muhammad pbuh, since they became Muslims, to suspect a Muslim of lying about Muhammad pbuh at that time was to accuse them of disbelief because Muhammad pbuh himself taught that those who lie about him should prepare for their place in the hellfire. Whereas Abu Musa (which was his nickname, Abdullah was his real name) was a well known trustworthy person. Yet Umar the ruler of the Muslims threatened to physically harm him with punishment for acting upon what he said he heard Muhammad pbuh teach him with his own two ears. Umar himself never even actually doubted Abu Musa but he did not want Muslims to think they could just say "Muhammad pbuh said X" and have it get believed without corroborating evidence as would be legally required in a court of law when giving testimony about what somebody had said. Legally Muslims who had lived with Muhammad pbuh were not allowed to even say what he taught them unless they could prove that he actually taught them what they claimed Muhammad pbuh taught them. Amongst the companions of Muhammad pbuh it was legally a punishable offense to just say "*Muhammad pbuh told me so*" the early generations of Muslims had to prove it, and this was even though they all knew that they had seen and heard Muhammad pbuh in the flesh. Obviously this is a very serious process of information verification that is the legal standard used throughout the world in courts today. Today many even sarcastically say "*Gee you don't have to make it a federal case*" when you ask for proof about something to back up what they say. Well for Muslims when it comes to saying that Muhammad pbuh said or taught something, it was always a federal case; literally. For someone known to have met Muhammad pbuh, for them to say something about Muhammad pbuh without proving what they said was true was considered to be a crime. If they couldn't prove what they claimed was true they would be convicted as criminals. The early Muslims took it as a matter of law to prove what they said about Muhammad pbuh was true because to have false information about a prophet of Allah circulate was too great a risk. To not have such strict requirements would imperil the entire religion. Without government policy making strict criteria for quotations and attributing teachings to prophets then there is no way to preserve the prophetic faith. The Jewish state was conquered by the Babylonians and their scriptures lost and corrupted, the Chirstians were persecuted for nearly 400 years before the heretical Christians took over Rome and caused the collapse of the Roman empire with sectarian infighting prior to Contstantine establishing a conglomeration of heretical Greek texts as Scripture that is still fine-tuned and edited until today. Simply put the task of preserving prophetic teachings from ancient times until today requires a government body sponsoring the prophetic faith and scrupulous scholastic students for generations and generations until widespread publishing became possible.

Verification of prophetic teachings and credentials of all the teachers inbetween the student and the prophet is obligatory. Is it a pain in the butt to do? Yes. But it must be done or else people will be able to change the religion with ease and without even being detected. Scholastically speaking there is no other way than this way. So this is "*the way to know what really happened in the past*", it has to have been a legal crime to not prove the past true from now all the way up to the past event one is referencing. One can only be able to prove the past if those past generations took this precaution in the past, unfortunately not every community has cared to diligently preserve the truth of their present while they were alive knowing that one day it would be the past. However this was the Muslim practice and standard after the prophet Muhammad pbuh. Umar actually declared the first principles for hadith to be:

1. The report should be literally faithful.

2. Every Hadith narrated should carry with it the name of the narrator and the chain of narrators.

3. The narrators must be of proven faith and integrity.

4. In judging the veracity of a report the occasion and circumstances involved should be taken into consideration.

5. The report cannot be repugnant/contradictory to Quran.

6. The report should be rational.

It still remains the legal religious standard but over time some Muslims became lax and then people said stuff without fully proving it and some made stuff up. This is when hadith qualities began to differ. For the first 3 generations there were only authentic hadiths and the isnads or chains of narrators were short. Such as Abu Musa's chain was a direct personal connection to Muhammad pbuh and he would be person A with Umar being person B. Yet when time passes and people get added on to that chain later then it can cause problems if those later people aren't considered trustworthy or reliable. This is because an unreliable person can relate something that's proven to be true and is 100% authentic, however because of their personal lack of credibility it tarnishes the trustworthiness of the information itself. A good example of this is the internet. If you say "*I learned on the internet....*" it's only natural that people are skeptical about such information just because of the source you learned it from even though the information may be completely trustworthy. Thus as a result of more links in the chains of narrators being added through time and the criteria that each chain in the link of narration has to be known as a reliable source, some hadith which were and are 100% true and authentic cannot in our modern day be labeled or classified as 100% authentic because our chain of information may not be 100% reliable or preserved to a high degree of precision. This is also because the principles of the science of hadith have evolved to be more strict to ensure authenticity, today the criteria is stricter because there is more information in the chain and the liars have evolved their lies as well. Anyone who sees a physical chain can understand this, in that 2 links are hard to separate from each other yet a chain with many links can easily be broken. As a result, today some hadith which are not classified as 100% true could be true, but legally we cannot say that they are because of the strict criteria of proving the truth. But don't get the wrong idea. There are thousands of authentic hadith who's chain is rock-solid 100% reliable and true who have been precisely preserved to a high degree. I'm just saying this because some people may incorrectly think that a "Good" or "Weak" hadith is automatically false because it's not labeled as Sahih or authentic. It is incorrect to think this. However legally from a religious perspective, even though a "Good" or "Weak" hadith may contain true information, such information alone cannot be used to justify a religious belief or action. What this means is that if someone says "*in X hadith it says.....*" and X hadith is classified as weak then the hadith could be true but you can't use that to justify believing or doing what it teaches. The hadith's grade would not be high enough to pass the test of usability. It's interesting information to ponder, or speculate about, but it's not very useful, in a practical sense. Unfortunately some Muslims don't understand this legal standard and they do things thinking it's okay to do because they learned it from a hadith of Muhammad pbuh. Whereas they forget that a "Weak" hadith means "It might NOT be true", so it's for safety reasons that one only follows 100% authentic information. It's a foolproof system, where if you can't prove it to be true then you can't legally use it as a religious proof, or else you'd be a fool. Such a method may seem strict but it's safe and legally necessary, because God will ask us why we believed what we believed and why we did what we did and you don't want to be basing your religion on something that "might be true". If it was that important to know or practice then God would've preserved such information with 100% authenticity. There is so much authentic information that one can live an entire lifetime without learning it all, so in general it is dangerous and needless to look into weak hadith. So for that reason I have limited my compilation of hadith that defeat the antichrist to Sahih and Hasan hadith only. Also I omitted isnads and limited myself to quoting from Hadith collections that are well known citing the source so the more advanced reader who is interested in and can benefit from the isnad can check the original sources for reference.

There is a common claim that if you get a row of twenty people and whisper one thing in the ear of one person on the end and tell them to pass it on then by the time it gets to the person on the other end it will be different than what you said as it gets changed through transmission. People try this and see it work out so they think it's impossible to ever know the truth of the past through oral transmission. However this argument is baseless and incorrect despite the real-world test seeming to match the hypothesis. First of all regarding the hadith or anything for that matter, nobody is whispering as they do in the chain game transmission test. Regarding the transmission of things in real life people speak aloud and clarify what they heard multiple times to ensure they remember it 100% correctly before passing it on and they write it down as well. This isn't done during the chain game transmission test so of course you will get different results if people are whispering and can't repeat themselves or write it down or take their time when transmitting information. Also the chain game test uses the general populace which makes the test invalid because the general populace is never used for oral transmission. Typically only those with impeccable character and prodigious memory are given such a responsibility. Whereas if you were to play the chain game with people who have great memories, speak clearly and seriously think that if they mess up the transmission they will be attributing a falsehood to God or a prophet of God and thus go to hell forever then you will get different results. For example teachers sometimes play the chain game in classes for fun with the original saying getting distorted. But imagine if the teacher told the kids that if the original saying gets distorted then every kid in the chain will fail the class. Would they get the same results? No. Likewise if the teacher made sure that they had each transmitter also whisper in their ear what they heard and what they said so the teacher could monitor each link in the chain and stipulated that only those who mess up the transmission of what they heard and said would fail would the same results be had? No. However some may ignorantly argue that no matter what there will always be a weak link in the chain preventing accurate transmission. This is the claim some may make with authentic hadith by saying Person C is a weak link in the isnad so it can't be trusted or graded as authentic. But Muhammad pbuh was no fool to only transmit his teachings to 1 person, he told many. So while one could say that person C in a chain is weak, what if you have 5 different chains which all say the same exact thing? Person C being weak would only discount 1 chain so then there would still be 4 chains free of person C that would require refuting in order to reject a teaching of the prophet. Hence the more reports there are the less likely they are unreliable if they all agree especially if the narrators in each chain never met together and conspiracy would be impossible. For instance lets say every class in the school gets told by the principal a special phrase to transmit via the chain game and are told that if they correctly transmit it they will get rewarded. Each class gets told the same thing for oral transmission and are not allowed to speak to other students. Now is it possible that every class will correctly transmit the phrase 100% intact? Yes, it is. Is it possible that some classes will mess up while others will succeed? Yes. Now is it possible for every class to fail to correctly transmit? Yes, in theory but it is highly unlikely and it is even more unlikely if the students at this school are intellectual elites with great memories and skills in oral transmission and truly care about correctly transmitting. Now to make it more like real life oral transmission one could do the following experiment. In his office a principal tells all the teachers in the school the message XYZ is to be orally transmitted via isnad. In class A Teacher #1 empties the classroom and has Student A1 come in and out loud tells the the hadith XYZ from the principal until the student learns it. After Student A1 learns it then Student A2 comes in and Student A1 reports "Teacher #1 told me the principal told her: "XYZ" pass it on along with the isnad. Then Teacher #1 leaves the room (simulating death) and Student A3 enters while it is Student A2's job to transmit. Student A2 says "Student A1 told me the teacher was told by the principal: XYZ" pass it on with the isnad. Then Student A1 leaves the room symbolizing death while Student A4 comes in to learn from Student A3 and on and on with the incoming student being able to confirm with the previous 2 students since the previous 2 generations are typically still alive to be consulted as confirmation for their part in the isnad. Now if every Teacher #1-26 used this method and every class did this it is entirely feasible to expect that every student would learn that the Principal said XYZ even though the Principal only told the Teachers XYZ and the majority of students would have learned it only from students and not the teachers much less the principal. This is how we are able to learn from God or a prophet without ever directly learning from God or a prophet. However isn't is possible for some students to mess up the transmission? Yes. It is because of this possibility for the narrators to theoretically mess up that there are multiple isnads for hadith. Imagine the Principal as Muhammad pbuh and the teachers of classes are his companions. None of the teachers (companions), would lie about what the principal said to pass on but the students(later Muslims) could make mistakes. However due to the large number and care taken the probability for accurate transmission becomes a near certainty and by having so many chains of transmission it eliminates the ability for someone to reject something the principal/prophet said simply because they have a problem with a student(narrator) or a particular chain of transmission (class). Some chains/isnads could be faulty but as a whole this method of oral transmission is reliable if done with care by intellectuals. Thus the claim *"It's impossible to ever know what someone in the past said through oral transmission."* is invalid if oral transmission is done in a methodologically correct manner by trustworthy individuals. Islam uses this method as well as the method of writing, other religions have not used this method since the times of their prophet, but Muslims have. Is it the ideal best manner? Maybe not but at the end of the day is there any better way for people in the 600s to have accurately conveyed information from Muhammad pbuh to us? Really lets consider those people met someone they believed was a prophet and believed they had to accurately convey his teachings to us today living thousands of years later. With the technology available to them what else could they have done which they didn't do? Every honest person must accept the fact that the scientific method of hadith is sound and the most realistic way for teachings to be accurately conveyed throughout history to the modern day and that to merely dismiss hadith as impossible to be true simply because Muhammad pbuh has been dead for so long is academically bigoted. It is 100% possible that Muslims have accurately preserved 100% of the teachings of Muhammad pbuh via oral transmission and writing. Any who claim otherwise are simply arrogant, ignorant bigots. Everyone who studies Quran and Hadith, whether they believe in Islam or not, agrees that it is exactly letter for letter the same today as what Muhammad originally disseminated.

There were only about 1,060 companions of Muhammad pbuh who reported hadith. Of which 500 of those 1,060 only reported 1 hadith. So 47% of the people who met Muhammad pbuh and reported hadith from him only adds up to 500 hadith, however the total number of authentic hadith is more because the other 560 sahabah who reported hadith reported more than just 1 hadith. Whereas you don't need to have a photogenic memory to accurately remember and report 1 hadith from Muhammad pbuh, so it's not as though every Sahabah who reported hadith was a genius master at memorization. 500 Sahabis only reported a single hadith. Some reported 2, some reported more than 2, some reported more than 10, while some companions of Muhammad pbuh reported 20+ hadith and seven noteworthy individuals reported more than a thousand each, although to be fair even these companions have some repeats amongst them where they both reported the same incident from their perspective. The companions in the thousand + reported club are Abu Hurairah, Abdullah bin Umar, Anas bin Malik, Aisha bint Abi Bakr, Abdullah ibn Abbas, Jabir bin Abdullah and Abu Said Al Khudri. The vast majority of the hadith were written down by the Sahabah during the lifetime of Muhammad pbuh. The individual man who reported the most hadith was Abu Hurairah. The woman who reported the most was Aisha (Muhammad's wife). Unfortunately there are two extremes with some thinking there are so many different authentic hadith reports that it's too much to learn or too much to be authentic and others think it's too few to be true or all-encompassing for everything one needs to know for life. Whereas it's neither too much nor too little and the hadith explain what sources to use if anything is not found in the hadith directly. Basically the Quran teaches that is has the answers and any answer not in the Quran can be found in the authentic hadith. The authentic hadith have the answers the Quran doesn't elaborate/enumerate and refers people to the companions of the prophet known as Sahabah, the Sahabah's companions known as the Tabieen and the companions of the Tabieen known as theTabi-Tabieen, for any extra information and for the correct explanation of the Quran and Sunnah. Those 3 generations are known as the Salaf. Both the Quran and authentic hadith also establish rules for deriving the correct analysis and rules from the Quran, authentic hadith, and the Salaf. Such principles include Ijma (consensus of the companions, the Salaf, the scholars, or the Muslims as a whole) as well as Qiyas (analogy). However Ijma and Qiyas are 4th and 5th regarding the sources of Shariah. #1 is the Quran, #2 is the Sunnah of Muhammad pbuh(found in the authentic hadith), #3 is the Salaf, #4 Ijma, #5 Qiyas. Sadly some mistakenly take Qiyas and put it in a higher rank than it is allowed to go in. Or they will mistake something as Ijma when it is not or think

that the Ijma of the past is the same as the Ijma at
the particular masjid they go to in the modern era,
or mistakenly think that the Ijma of the past is the
same as the Ijma of the Salaf. Others foolishly and
blasphemously go out of order thinking Qiyas is #1
then Quran is #2 or any other kind of mixed up
order contrary to the order Allah and Muhammad
pbuh taught us. Others incorrectly limit the
numbers of sources and will ignorantly say things
like Qiyas is all I need or the Quran is all one needs,
not realizing that the Quran itself says one needs to
follow/know #2-5 too. Though fundamentally if
you follow the Quran and Sunnah that's all you
need but technically and in reality the 3rd, 4th and
5th components of Islam are subcategories of the
Quran and Sunnah. Technically the Sunnah is a
subcategory of the Quran too but because there is a
deviant heretical sect that takes only the Quran and
rejects the Sunnah thinking the Quran is all they
need then I'm not going to say that because they
would mistake it without understanding that
following the Quran involves following the Sunnah
which involves following the Companions and Salaf
which involves following Ijma and occasionally
using Qiyas when appropriate. Such people are
called Quranites and are as foolish as a Jew saying

all they need is "the Law of Moses" and to stick to the book so any hadith/statement of Moses pbuh they reject it since they only follow "the Law of Moses". Whereas anyone can see such a methodology is preposterous and silly but perhaps they might not because there are no authentic hadith of Moses pbuh which have survived transmission to this day. Likewise there are no authentic hadith of Jesus that have survived to this day. So Muhammad is truly the only claimant to traditional ancient prophethood who we can reliably confidently prove we have information from. Thus despite believing in the prior prophets of God and their prophecies I have not found any authentic information from them pertaining to the antichrist to use for this book. So only Muhammadean hadith have been utilized in this book since that's the only material that we can use scholastically speaking.

The true monotheist is not merely someone who believes in one God but is someone who believes in and worships the one unique true God correctly upon prophetic knowledge, speech and actions; daily until their death. Some idolator who only worships one statue is not a true monotheist because in worshipping a false god though the number is restricted to one they are invariably worshipping their own desires and lusts in contradiction to the teachings of the prophets. Thus people must beware of self-worship that pollutes their lifestyle for just as Jews and Christians are guilty of worshipping Rabbis and Priests by obeying them in legalizing what God forbade and forbidding what God allowed, many others do the same thing on a daily basis. Television for example is cited by many as having some link to the antichrist but such a link is fictious and unnecessary for one to know the majority of television programs are forbidden. Yet despite knowing that most television programs are forbidden due to the sins of lying/acting, indecent dress codes, idle talk, music, lewd speech, anti-prophetic immoral teachings and actions glorifying disbelief in God and sinfulness as a way of life and serving as a waste of our precious lifespan, how many are willing to live life without television as a safety precaution? It is well-known how corrupting television is yet people persist on the poison citing miniscule chance of worldly benefit despite drowning in the sins of cinematography while at the same time such people think when the antichrist comes then he will be a minor challenge to them because their faith is so strong. In reality if you got a television in your house, chances are you watch sinful stuff on it, and chances are that should the antichrist emerge you would fail the test because you can't even resist a opportunity to sin with television. Truly they need not worry about losing to the antichrist because the devil already beat them with a television. One can apply this comparison to every sin one is exposed to, especially innovators and people of false religions. Voting is another example wherein it is easy to see how someone who can't resist the myths of the religion of democracy and voluntarily partake in the ritual of voting for evil when the prophetic faith forbids it will have little resolve to resist following the antichrist politically. If you are interfaith and tolerant as modern politics dictates as just and wise then this is another sign of impending doom, for if you can't even be intolerant and emphatic upon the prophetic creed and methodology in pre-antichrist times then you have nearly no chance during post-antichrist times. For the antichrist and his followers will come with evidences including miraculous feats and claims of monotheism. For after all if they all worship the antichrist only, then technically according to the dictionaries that is a type of monotheism since they aren't worshipping multiple things but just one. Trinitarian Christians are actually less entitled to claim monotheism because they worship 3, a God, a son of God and a Ghost/Spirit, apparently all equally though they never pray 33% to each because in reality its all 100% following the desires of false preachers who themselves followed false preachers whom they know nearly nothing about except for the myths they pass down to each other. Hence falsehood has its own chain of narration too in order to pass on evil from one generation to the next, though it is ever diluting in nature in contrast to the prophetic faith which remains exactly the same throughout the various eras without change.

Thus the intolerance for worshipping according to non-prophetic creeds and methodologies is a safety buffer against the doubts and deceptions of disbelievers in every era. The modernist Interfaith pluralist progressive notion is basically the antichrist's religion anyways because the antichrist unites all falsehood together so that everyone agrees except the genuine followers of the prophets. So disunity between the people of truth and people of falsehood must be made distinct because without such distinction there will only be contamination and corruption due to confusion. If you want to be friends with everybody then you got no business being friends with God, since God forbids taking his enemies as other than enemies. Whereas God prepared hell for his enemies and his sinful friends so alliances are not something to take lightly when even true monotheists can spend some time in hell if they fail to repent properly before they die. To think you can remain as sinful as you are today without improving and that you'd be safe even if the antichrist emerged in your lifetime is foolishness. Treat every sin as it truly is. Sin is disobedience to your Creator and obedience to Satan who is a more severe enemy than the antichrist. So if you are losing to Satan on a daily basis then you're already losing and the antichrist would just seal the deal for Satan's designs for you and it is a mercy from God that you haven't been exposed to the antichrist. Yet that doesn't get you off the hook of responsibility for waging war against the antichrist because such a job is the job of every generation. As stated before the primary tool the generation that opposes the antichrist will have to fight with is the hadith or prophetic reports so they can recognize the truth from falsehood and the safety from the harm. We have these precious reports available in our era in abundance with ease of access but the situation may not be that way for long. Hence we must take advantage of the blessings we have today to prepare for the times of hardship and trials. Therefore it is only fit that as a claimant to the prophetic belief and methodology I pass on as best I can the teachings pertaining to the antichrist so I better learn them and get credit for teaching my family and acquaintances as well as anyone who comes across this information I compile. It is a duty on every slave of God to warn the world and the future creatures of what is impending for the benefit of both the warner and the warned. Such is what the prophetic faith entails. If you haven't fought against the antichrist then you need to because you don't want to meet God without any medals of honor for having passed on reports pertaining to God's enemies. Even if it is just a single authentic prophetic report you teach once in your lifetime to another creature then that will count as goodness to your credit and make you a soldier against Satan and the antichrist. That rule applies moreso against Satan than the antichrist because Satan is a higher level enemy than the antichrist. Whereas while this book focuses on the antichrist others exist that report on defeating Satan so you can read and learn to protect yourself against Satan and fight against him too, instead of getting programmed by satanic television, music or other evil things. Anything you teach of the genuine prophetic faith intending to defeat the plethora of satanic innovations and lifestyles then it marks you as a soldier of God against Satan and his soldiers, so in whatever capacity you are capable of the best deed you can do is to imitate the prophets and teach others about the true prophetic faith while practicing it sincerely yourself. That is the most rewarding deed and indeed the most needed in every era. In reality the majority of people die before the emergence of the antichrist yet people of all eras can get credit for fighting against him, so I write this as an incitement to recruitment for the army against Satan and the antichrist because the summary of the prophetic faith is defined as:

 To worship the true singular Creator of everything exclusively according to how his prophets taught while rejecting and opposing Satan and all who disbelieve and distort the prophetic creed and methodology, until we die.

HADITH THAT DEFEAT THE ACCURSED ANTICHRIST KNOWN AS AD-DAJJAL

Abu Sa`id al-Khudri reported:

We came back after having performed Pilgrimage or `Umra and Ibn Sa'id was along with us. And we encamped at a place and the people dispersed and I and he were left behind. I felt terribly frightened from him as it was said about him that he was the Dajjal. He brought his goods and placed them by my luggage and I said: It is intense heat. Would you not place that under that tree? And he did that. Then there appeared before us a flock of sheep. He went and brought a cup of milk and said: Abu Sa`id, drink that. I said it is intense heat and the milk is also hot (whereas the fact was) that I did not like to drink from his hands or to take it from his hand and he said: Abu Sa`id, I think that I should take a rope and suspend it by the tree and then commit suicide because of the talks of the people, and he further said. Abu Sa`id he who is ignorant of the saying of Allah's Messenger (ﷺ) (he is to be pardoned), but O people of Ansar, is this hadith of Allah's Messenger (ﷺ) concealed from you whereas you have the best knowledge of the hadith of Allah's Messenger (ﷺ) amongst people? Did Allah's Messenger (ﷺ) not say that he (Dajjal) would be a non-believer whereas I am a believer? Did Allah's Messenger (ﷺ) not say he would be barren and no child would be born to him, whereas I have left my children in Medina? Did Allah's Messenger (may peace upon him) not say: He would not get into Medina and Mecca whereas I have been coming from Medina and now I intend to go to Mecca? Abu Sa`id said: I was about to accept the excuse put forward by him. Then he said: I know the place where he would be born and where he is now. So I said to him: May your whole day be spent.

Source: Sahih Muslim 2927c

Narrated Ibn 'Umar:

Umar and a group of the companions of the Prophet (ﷺ) set out with the Prophet to Ibn Saiyad. He found him playing with some boys near the hillocks of Bani Maghala. Ibn Saiyad at that time was nearing his puberty. He did not notice (the Prophet's presence) till the Prophet (ﷺ) stroked him on the back with his hand and said, "Ibn Saiyad! Do you testify that I am Allah's Messenger (ﷺ)?" Ibn

Saiyad looked at him and said, "I testify that you are the Apostle of the illiterates."

Then Ibn Saiyad asked the Prophet. "Do you testify that I am the apostle of Allah?" The Prophet (ﷺ) said to him, "I believe in Allah and His Apostles." Then the Prophet (ﷺ) said (to Ibn Saiyad). "What do you see?" Ibn Saiyad replied, "True people and false ones visit me." The Prophet said, "Your mind is confused as to this matter." The Prophet (ﷺ) added, " I have kept something (in my mind) for you." Ibn Saiyad said, "It is Ad-Dukh." The Prophet (ﷺ) said (to him), "Shame be on you! You cannot cross your limits." On that 'Umar said, "O Allah's Messenger (ﷺ)! Allow me to chop his head off." The Prophet (ﷺ) said, "*If he should be him (i.e. Ad-Dajjal) then you cannot overpower him, and should he not be him, then you are not going to benefit by murdering him.*"

Source: Sahih al-Bukhari 3055

Abu Hurairah narrated that the Messenger of Allah said:

"*The Hour shall not be established until nearly thirty imposters, Dajjal appear, each of them claiming that he is the Messenger of Allah.*"

Source: Jami` at-Tirmidhi 2218 Grade: Sahih

Imran bin Hussain reported:

I heard the Messenger of Allah (ﷺ) saying, "*Between time of the creation of Adam and the Resurrection Day, there is nothing greater than the mischief of Dajjal (the Antichrist).*"

Source: Riyad as-Salihin 1814 Grade: Sahih

Ibn `Umar reported:

We were talking about the Farewell Pilgrimage without knowing what was it when Messenger of Allah (ﷺ) was also present. He (ﷺ) stood up and recited the Praise and Glorification of Allah. He then gave a detailed account of Ad-Dajjal and said, '*Every Prophet sent by Allah had warned his people against his mischief. Nuh (ﷺ))warned his nation and so did all the Prophets after him. If he (i.e., Ad-Dajjal) appears among you, his condition will not remain hidden from you. Your Rubb is not one-eyed, but Ad-Dajjal is. His right eye is protruding like a swollen grape. Listen, Allah has made your blood, and your properties as inviolable as of this day of yours (i.e., the Day of Sacrifice), in this city of yours (i.e., Makkah), in this month of yours (i.e., Dhul -Hijjah). Listen, have I conveyed Allah's Message to you?*'' The people replied in affirmative. There upon he said, "*O Allah, bear witness.*''

And he repeated it thrice. He (ﷺ) concluded: "Do not revert after me as infidels killing one another".

Source: Riyad as-Salihin 205 Grade: Sahih

Narrated `Abdullah bin `Umar:

Allah's Messenger (ﷺ) stood up amongst the people and then praised and glorified Allah as He deserved and then he mentioned Ad-Dajjal, saying, *"I warn you of him, and there was no prophet but warned his followers of him; but I will tell you something about him which no prophet has told his followers: Ad- Dajjal is one-eyed whereas Allah is not."*

Source: Sahih al-Bukhari 7127

Ibn Umar reported that Allah's Messenger (ﷺ). made a mention of Dajjal in the presence of the people and said:

Allah is not one-eyed and behold that Dajjal is blind of the right eye and his eye would be like a floating grape.

Source: Sahih Muslim 169e

Narrated `Abdullah:

Ad-Dajjal was mentioned in the presence of the Prophet. The Prophet (ﷺ) said, *"Allah is not hidden from you; He is not one-eyed,"* and pointed with his hand towards his eye, adding, *"While Al-Masih Ad- Dajjal is blind in the right eye and his eye looks like a protruding grape."*

Source: Sahih al-Bukhari 7407

Narrated Anas:

The Prophet (ﷺ) said, *"Allah did not send any prophet but that he warned his nation of the one-eyed liar (Ad-Dajjal). He is one-eyed while your Lord is not one-eyed, The word 'Kafir' (unbeliever) is written between his two eyes."*

Source: Sahih al-Bukhari 7408

It was narrated from Jabir bin Samurah, that Nafi' bin 'Utbah bin Abu Waqqas narrated that the Prophet (ﷺ) said:

"You will fight the Arabian Peninsula and victory will be granted by Allah. Then you will fight the Romans and victory will be granted (by Allah). Then you will fight Dajjal and victory will be granted (by Allah)." Jabir said: "Dajjal will not appear until you have fought the Romans."

Source: Sunan Ibn Majah 4091 Grade: Sahih

Abu Huraira reported Allah's Messenger (ﷺ) as saying:

*The Last Hour would not come until the Romans would
land at al-A'maq or in Dabiq. An army consisting of the
best (soldiers) of the people of the earth at that time will
come from Medina (to counteract them). When they will
arrange themselves in ranks, the Romans would say: Do
not stand between us and those (Muslims) who took
prisoners from amongst us. Let us fight with them; and
the Muslims would say: Nay, by Allah, we would never
get aside from you and from our brethren that you may
fight them. They will then fight and a third (part) of the
army would run away, whom Allah will never forgive. A
third (part of the army) which would be constituted of
excellent martyrs in Allah's eye, would be killed and the
third who would never be put to trial would win and
they would be conquerors of Constantinople. And as they
would be busy in distributing the spoils of war (amongst
themselves) after hanging their swords by the olive trees,
the Satan would cry: The Dajjal has taken your place
among your family. They would then come out, but it
would be of no avail. And when they would come to
Syria, he would come out while they would be still
preparing themselves for battle drawing up the ranks.
Certainly, the time of prayer shall come and then Jesus
(peace be upon him) son of Mary would descend and
would lead them. When the enemy of Allah would see
him, it would (disappear) just as the salt dissolves itself
in water and if he (Jesus) were not to confront them at*

*all, even then it would dissolve completely, but Allah
would kill them by his hand and he would show them
their blood on his lance (the lance of Jesus Christ).*

Source: Sahih Muslim 2897

Abu Huraira reported Allah's Apostle saying:

*You have heard about a city, one side of which is on land
and the other is in the sea (Constantinople).* They said:
Allah's Messenger, yes. Thereupon he said: *The Last
Hour would not come unless seventy thousand persons
from Bani Ishaq would attack it. When they would land
there, they will neither fight with weapons nor would
shower arrows but would only say: "There is no god but
Allah and Allah is the Greatest," and one side of it would
fall. Thaur (one of the narrators) said: I think that he
said: The part by the side of the ocean. Then they would
say for the second time: "There is no god but Allah and
Allah is the Greatest" and the second side would also fall,
and they would say: "There is no god but Allah and
Allah is the Greatest," and the gates would be opened for
them and they would enter therein and, they would be
collecting spoils of war and distributing them amongst
themselves when a noise would be heard saying: Verily,
Dajjal has come. And thus they would leave everything
there and go back.*

Source: Sahih Muslim 2920a

Yusair bin Jabir reported:

Once there blew a red storm in Kufah that there came a person who had nothing to say but (these words): `Abdullah bin Mas`ud, the Last Hour has come. He (`Abdullah bin Mas`ud) was sitting reclining against something, and he said: The Last Hour would not come until shares of inheritance are not distributed and there is no rejoicing over spoils of war. Then he said pointing towards Syria, with the gesture of his hand like this: The enemy shall muster strength against Muslims and the Muslims will muster strength against them (Syrians). I said: You mean Rome? And he said: Yes, and there would be a terrible fight and the Muslims would prepare a detachment (for fighting unto death) which would not return but victorious. They will fight until night will intervene them; both the sides will return without being victorious and both will be wiped out. The Muslims will again prepare a detachment for fighting unto death so that they may not return but victorious. When it would be the fourth day, a new detachment out of the remnant of the Muslims would be prepared and Allah will decree that the enemy should be routed. And they would fight such a fight the like of which would not be seen, so much so that even if a bird were to pass their flanks, it would fall down dead before reaching the end of them. (There would be such a large scale massacre) that when counting would be done, (only) one out of a hundred men related to one another would be found alive. So what can be the joy at the spoils of such war and what inheritance would be divided! They would be in this very state that they would hear of a calamity more horrible than this. And a cry would reach them: The Dajjal has taken your place among your offspring. They will, therefore, throw away what would be in their hands and go forward sending ten horsemen, as a scouting party. Allah's Messenger (ﷺ) said: *I know their names and the names of their forefathers and the color of their horses. They will be the best horsemen on the surface of the earth on that day or amongst the best horsemen on the surface of the earth on that day.*

Source: Sahih Muslim 2899a

Narrated Mu'adh ibn Jabal:

The Prophet (ﷺ) said: *The flourishing state of Jerusalem will be when Yathrib is in ruins, the ruined state of Yathrib will be when the great war comes, the outbreak of the great war will be at the conquest of Constantinople and the conquest of Constantinople when the Dajjal (Antichrist) comes forth. He (the Prophet) struck his thigh or his shoulder with his hand and said: This is as true as you are here or as you are sitting* (meaning Mu'adh ibn Jabal).

Source: Sunan Abi Dawud 4294 Grade: Hasan

Narrated Abdullah ibn Umar:

When we were sitting with the Messenger of Allah (ﷺ), he talked about periods of trial (fitnahs), mentioning many of them.

When he mentioned the one when people should stay in their houses, some asked him: Messenger of Allah, what is the trial (fitnah) of staying at home?

He replied: *It will be flight and plunder. Then will come a test which is pleasant. Its murkiness is due to the fact that it is produced by a man from the people of my house, who will assert that he belongs to me, whereas he does not, for my friends are only the God-fearing. Then the people will unite under a man who will be like a hip-bone on a rib. Then there will be the little black trial which will leave none of this community without giving him a slap, and when people say that it is finished, it will be extended. During it a man will be a believer in the morning and an infidel in the evening, so that the people will be in two camps: the camp of faith which will contain no hypocrisy, and the camp of hypocrisy which will contain no faith. When that happens, expect the Antichrist (Dajjal) that day or the next.*

Source: Sunan Abi Dawud 4242 Grade: Sahih

It was narrated from Ibn 'Umar that:

The Messenger of Allah said: "*There will emerge people who will recite the Qur'an but it will not go any deeper than their collarbones. Whenever a group of them appears, they should be cut off (i.e. killed)." Ibn 'Umar said: "I heard the Messenger of Allah say: 'Whenever a group of them appears, they should be killed' - (he said it) more than twenty times- 'until Dajjal emerges among them.'*"

Source: Sunan Ibn Majah 174 Grade: Hasan

It was narrated that Sharik bin Shihab said:

"I used to wish that I could meet a man among the Companions of the Prophet and ask him about the Khawarij. Then I met Abu Barzah on the day of 'Id, with a number of his companions. I said to him: 'Did you hear the Messenger of Allah mention the Khawarij?' He said: 'Yes. I heard the Messenger of Allah with my own ears, and saw him with my own eyes. Some wealth was brought to the Messenger of Allah and he distributed it to those on his right and on his left, but he did not give anything to those who were behind him. Then a man stood behind him and said: "O Muhammad! You have not been just in your division!" He was a man with black patchy (shaved) hair, wearing two white garments. So Allah's Messenger became very angry and said: *"By Allah! You will not find a man after me who is more just than me."* Then he said: *"A people will come at the end of time; as if he is one of them, reciting the Qur'an without it passing beyond their throats. They will go through Islam just as the arrow goes through the target. Their distinction will be shaving. They will not cease to appear until the last of them comes with Al-Masih Ad-Dajjal. So when you meet them, then kill them, they are the worst of created beings."*

Source: Sunan an-Nasa'i 4103 Grade: Hasan

Nafi' bin Utba reported:

We were with Allah's Messenger (ﷺ) in an expedition that there came a people to Allah's Apostle (ﷺ) from the direction of the west. They were dressed in woollen clothes and they stood near a hillock and they met him as Allah's Messenger (ﷺ) was sitting. I said to myself: Better go to them and stand between him and them that they may not attack him. Then I thought that perhaps there had been going on secret negotiation amongst them. I however, went to them and stood between them and him and I remember four of the words (on that occasion) which I repeat (on the fingers of my hand) that he (Allah's Messenger) said: *You will attack Arabia and Allah will enable you to conquer it, then you would attack Persia and He would make you to conquer it. Then you would attack Rome and Allah will enable you to conquer it, then you would attack the Dajjal and Allah will enable you to conquer him. Nafi' said: Jabir, we thought that the Dajjal would appear after Rome (Syrian territory) would be conquered.*

Source: Sahih Muslim 2900

Anas bin Malik reported that Allah's Messenger (ﷺ) said:

The Dajjal would be followed by seventy thousand Jews of Isfahan wearing Persian shawls.

Source: Sahih Muslim 2944

It was narrated that Abu Bakr Siddiq said:

"The Messenger of Allah (ﷺ) told us: *'Dajjal will emerge in a land in the east called Khorasan, and will be followed by people with faces like hammered shields.'*"

Source: Sunan Ibn Majah 4072 Grade: Hasan

Narrated Umm Sharik:

that the Messenger of Allah (ﷺ) said: "*The people will flee from the Dajjal such that they will go to the mountains.*" Umm Sharik said: "O Messenger of Allah! Where will the Arabs be that day?" He said: "*They will be few.*"

Source: Jami` at-Tirmidhi 3930 Grade: Sahih

Narrated Abu Huraira:

I have not ceased to like Banu Tamim ever since I heard of three qualities attributed to them by Allah's Messenger (ﷺ) (He said): *They, out of all my followers, will be the strongest opponent of Ad-Dajjal;* `Aisha had a slave-girl from them, and the Prophet (ﷺ) told her to manumit her as she was from the descendants of (the Prophet) Ishmael; and, when their Zakat was brought, the Prophet (ﷺ) said, "This is the Zakat of my people."

Source: Sahih al-Bukhari 4366

Narrated Ibn `Abbas:

The Prophet (ﷺ) said, "*On the night of my Ascent to the Heaven, I saw Moses who was a tall brown curly haired man as if he was one of the men of Shan'awa tribe, and I saw Jesus, a man of medium height and moderate complexion inclined to the red and white colors and of lank hair. I also saw Malik, the gate-keeper of the (Hell)*

Fire and Ad-Dajjal amongst the signs which Allah showed me." (The Prophet then recited the Holy Verse): "So be not you in doubt of meeting him' when you met Moses during the night of Mi'raj over the heavens" (32.23) Narrated Anas and Abu Bakra: "The Prophet (ﷺ) said, "The angels will guard Medina from Ad-Dajjal (who will not be able to enter the city of Medina).

Source: Sahih al-Bukhari 3239

Narrated Abu Hurairah:

that the Prophet (ﷺ) said: "There are three, for which when they appear, a soul will not benefit by its faith, if it did not believe before the Signs: Ad-Dajjal, the Beast, and the rising of the sun from its setting place" - or "from the west."

Source: Jami` at-Tirmidhi 3072 Grade: Sahih

Anas bin Malik reported that Allah's Messenger (ﷺ) said:

Dajjal is blind of one eye and there is written between his eyes the word" Kafir". He then spelled the word as k. f. r., which every Muslim would be able to read.

Source: Sahih Muslim 2933c

Anas said:

The Messenger of Allah (ﷺ) said, "*There has not been a Prophet who has not warned his Ummah of that one-eyed liar (Dajjal). Behold, he is blind in one eye and your Rubb (Allah) is not blind. On his forehead are the letters: (K.F.R.) (meaning Kafir- disbeliever).*"

Source: Riyad as-Salihin 1817 Grade: Sahih

It is narrated on the authority of 'Abdulldh bin Umar that one day the Messenger of Allah (ﷺ) mentioned in the presence of people about al-Masih al-Dajjal. He said:

Verily Allah (hallowed be He and High) is not blind of one eye. Behold, but the Masih al-Dajjal is blind of right eye as if his eye is like a swollen grape, and the Messenger of Allah (ﷺ) said: I was shown in a dream in the night that near the Ka'bah there was a man fair-complexioned, fine amongst the white-complexioned men that you ever saw, his locks of hair were falling on his shoulders. He was a man whose hair were neither too curly nor too straight, and water trickled down from his head. He was placing his bands on the shoulders of two persons and amidst them was making a circuit around the Ka'bah. I said: Who is he? They replied: Al-Masih son of Mary. And I saw behind him a man with intensely curly hair, blind of right eye. Amongst the persons I have ever seen Ibn Qatan has the greatest resemblance with him. He was making a circuit around the Ka'bah by placing both his hands on the shoulders of two persons. I said: Who is he? They said; It is al-Masih al-Dajjal.

Source: Sahih Muslim 169b

Anas bin Malik said:

The Messenger of Allah (ﷺ) said, "*There will be no land which will not be trampled by Dajjal (the Antichrist) but Makkah and Al-Madinah; and there will be no passage leading to them which will not be guarded by the angels, arranged in rows. Dajjal will appear in a barren place adjacent to Al- Madinah and the city will be shaken three times. Allah will expel from it every disbeliever and hypocrite.*"

Source: Riyad as-Salihin 1811 Grade: Sahih

Fatimah, daughter of Qais, said:

I heard the crier of the Messenger of Allah calling: Assemble for the prayer. I Then came out and prayed along with the Messenger of Allah : When the Messenger of Allah finished his prayer, he sat on the pulpit laughing, and he said : Everyone should remain where he had said his prayer. He then asked : Do you know why I have assembled you? They said: Allah and His Messenger know best. He said: I did not call you together for some alarming news or for something good. Rather, I called you all because Tamim al-Dari, a Christian, who came and accepted Islam, told me something which agrees with what I was telling you about the Dajjal(Antichrist). He told me that he sailed with thirty men of Lakhm and Judham and that they were storm-tossed for a month. They drew near to an island when the sun was setting. They sat in a boat nearest to them and entered the island where they were met by a very hairy beast. They said: Woe to you! What can you be ? It replied : I am the Jassasah. Go to this man in the monastery, for he is anxious to get news of you. He said : When it named a man to us we were afraid of it lest it should be a she-devil. So we went off quickly and entered the monastery, where we found a man with the hugest and strongest frame we had ever seen with his hands chained to his neck. He then narrated the rest of the tradition. He asked them about the palm-trees of Baisan and the spring of Zughar and about the unlettered prophet. He said: I am the false-messiah (the Antichrist) and will be soon given permission to emerge. And the Prophet said: He is in the Syrian sea or the Yemeni sea: No, on the contrary, it is towards the east that he is. He said it twice and pointed his hand to the east. She said: I memorized this (tradition) from the Messenger of Allah, and she narrated the tradition.

Source: Sunan Abi Dawud 4326 Grade: Sahih

Amir bin Sharahil Sha'bi Sha'b Hamdan reported that he asked Fatima, daughter of Qais and sister of ad-Dahhak bin Qais and she was the first amongst the emigrant women:

Narrate to me a hadith which you had heard directly from Allah's Messenger and there is no extra link in between them. She said: Very well, if you like, I am prepared to do that, and he said to her: Well, do It and narrate that to me. She said: I married the son of Mughira and he was a chosen young man of Quraish at that time, but he fell as a martyr in the first Jihad (fighting) on the side of Allah's Messenger. When I became a widow, 'Abd al-Rahman bin Auf, one amongst the group of the Companions of Allah's Messenger, sent me the proposal of marriage. Allah's Messenger also sent me such a message for his freed slave Usama bin Zaid. And it had been conveyed to me that Allah's Messenger had said (about Usama): He who loves me should also love Usama. When Allah's Messenger talked to me (about this matter), I said: My affairs are in your hand. You may marry me to anyone whom you like. He said: You better shift now to the house of Umm Sharik, and Umm Sharik was a rich lady from amongst the Ansar. She spent generously for the cause of Allah and entertained guests very hospitably. I said: Well, I will do as you like. He said: Do not do that for Umm Sharik is a woman who is very frequently visited by guests and I do not like that your head may be uncovered or the cloth may be removed from your shank and the strangers may catch sight of them which you abhor. You better shift to the house of your cousin 'Abdullah bin 'Amr bin Umm Maktum and he is a person of the Bani Fihr branch of the Quraish, and he belonged to that tribe (to which Fatima) belonged. So I shifted to that house, and when my period of waiting was over, I heard the voice of an announcer making an announcement that the prayer would be observed in the mosque (where) congregational prayer (is observed). So I set out towards that mosque and observed prayer along with Allah's Messenger and I was in the row of the women which was near the row of men. When Allah's Messenger had finished his prayer, he sat on the pulpit smiling and said: Every worshipper should keep sitting at his place. He then said: Do you know why I had asked you to assemble? They said: Allah and His Messenger know best. He said: By Allah. I have not made you assemble for exhortation or for a warning, but I have detained you here, for Tamim Dari, a Christian, who came and accepted Islam, told me something, which agrees with what I was telling, you about the Dajjal(Antichrist). He narrated to me that he had sailed in a ship along with thirty men of Bani Lakhm and Bani Judham and had been tossed by waves in the ocean for a month. Then these (waves) took them (near) the land within the ocean (island) at the time of sunset. They sat

in a small side-boat and entered that island. There was a
beast with long thick hair (and because of these) they
could not distinguish his face from his back. They said:
Woe to you, who can you be? Thereupon it said: I am al-
Jassasa. They said: What is al-Jassasa? And it said: O
people, go to this person in the monastery as he is very
much eager to know about you. He (the narrator) said:
When it named a person for us we were afraid of it lest it
should be a devil. Then we hurriedly went on till we
came to that monastery and found a well-built person
there with his hands tied to his neck and having iron
shackles between his two legs up to the ankles. We said:
Woe be upon thee, who are you? And he said: You would
soon come to know about me. but tell me who are you.
We said: We are people from Arabia and we embarked
upon a boat but the sea-waves had been driving us for
one month and they brought as near this island. We got
into the side-boats and entered this island and here a
beast met us with profusely thick hair and because of the
thickness of his hair his face could not be distinguished
from his back. We said: Woe be to thee, who are you? It
said: I am al- Jassasa. We said: What is al-Jassasa? And
it said: You go to this very person in the monastery for he
is eagerly waiting for you to know about you. So we came
to you in hot haste fearing that that might be the Devil.
He (that chained person) said: Tell me about the date-
palm trees of Baisan. We said: About what aspect of

theirs do you seek information? He said: I ask you whether these trees bear fruit or not. We said: yes. Thereupon he said: I think these would not bear fruits. He said: Inform me about the lake of Tabariyya? We said: Which aspect of it do you want to know? He said: Is there water in it? They said: There is abundance of water in it. Thereupon he said: I think it would soon become dry. He again said: Inform me about the spring of Zughar. They said: Which aspect of it you want to know? He (the chained person) said: Is there water in it and does it irrigate (the land)? We said to him: Yes, there is abundance of water in it and the inhabitants (of Medina) irrigate (land) with the help of it, He said: Inform me about the unlettered Prophet; what has he done? We said: He has come out from Mecca and has settled In Yathrib (Medina). He said: Do the Arabs fight against him? We said: Yes. He said: How did he deal with them? We informed him that he had overcome those in his neighborhood and they had submitted themselves before him. Thereupon he said to us: Has it actually happened? We said: Yes. Thereupon he said: If it is so that is better for them that they should show obedience to him. I am going to tell you about myself and I am Dajjal(Anti-christ) and would be soon permitted to get out and so I shall get out and travel in the land, and will not spare any town where I would not stay for forty nights except Mecca and Medina as these two (places) are prohibited (areas) for me and I would not make an attempt to enter any one of these two. An angel with a sword in his hand would confront me and would bar my way and there would be angels to guard every passage leading to it; then Allah's Messenger striking the pulpit with the help of the end of his staff said: This implies Taiba meaning Medina. Have I not, told you an account (of the Dajjal) like this? 'The people said: Yes, and this account narrated by Tamim Dari was liked by me for it corroborates the account which I gave to you in regard to him (Dajjal) at Medina and Mecca. Behold he (Dajjal) is in the Syrian sea (Mediterranean) or the Yemen sea (Arabian sea). Nay, on the contrary, he is in the east, he is in the east, he is in the east, and he pointed with his hand towards the east. I (Fatima bint Qais) said: I preserved it in my mind (this narration from Allah's Messenger).

Source: Sahih Muslim 2942a

Abu Sa'id Al-Khudri reported:

I heard the Prophet (ﷺ) saying, "*Dajjal (the Antichrist) will come forth and a person from amongst the believers will go towards him and the armed watchmen of Dajjal will meet him and they will say to him: 'Where do you intend to go?' He will say: 'I intend to go to this one who has appeared.' They will say to him: 'Don't you believe in our lord (meaning Dajjal)?' He will say: 'There (i.e., we know Him to be Allah, Alone, without any partners) is nothing hidden about our Rubb.' Some of them will say: 'Let us kill him', but some others will say: 'Has your lord (Dajjal) not forbidden you to kill anyone without his consent?' So they will take him to Dajjal. When the believer will see him, he will say: 'O people! This is Dajjal about whom the Messenger of Allah (ﷺ) has informed us.' Dajjal will have him laid on his stomach and have his head. He will be struck on his back and on his stomach. Dajjal will ask him: 'Don't you believe in me?' He will say: 'You are the false Messiah.' He will then give his order to have him sawn with a saw into two from the parting of his hair up to his legs. After that Dajjal will walk between the two halves and will say to him: 'Stand up', and he will stand on his feet. He will then say to him: 'Don't you believe in me?' The person will say: 'It has added to my insight that you are Dajjal'. He will add: 'O people! He will not be able to behave with anyone amongst people in such a manner after me.' Dajjal will try to kill him. The space between his neck and collarbone will turn into copper and he will find no way to kill him. So he will catch hold of him by his hand and feet and throw him into (what appears to be the fire). The people will think that he has been thrown into the fire whereas he will be thrown into Jannah." The Messenger of Allah (ﷺ) added, "He will be the most eminent amongst the people with regard to martyrdom near the Lord of the worlds."*

Source: Riyad as-Salihin 1815 Grade: Sahih

The key lesson of this hadith is that the man twice martyred by the Dajjal will know of the Dajjal/Antichrist being such due to his knowledge of the hadith of Muhammad. How will the man have known the hadith when he is not a contemporary Sahabah of Muhammad? Because of people preserving and passing the hadith down generation to generation all the way to him. You can be part of that chain of narration of goodness. This hadith also shows the honor of the people of hadith for the man attributes the knowledge directly to the prophet and not his sheikh or Imam who he learned the hadith from because his methodology is that of ahl-hadith and thereby his true/only sheikh or Imam is the prophet Muhammad and everyone else is a fellow student. So this hadith shows the danger of the madhhab fanatics who blindly follow madhhabs in opposition to the hadith of the prophet. The best of martyrs and opponent of the Dajjal is upon the methodology of ahl-hadith or Salafi.

Narrated Abu Sa`id:

One day Allah's Messenger (ﷺ) narrated to us a long narration about Ad-Dajjal and among the things he narrated to us, was: "*Ad-Dajjal will come, and he will be forbidden to enter the mountain passes of Medina. He will encamp in one of the salt areas neighboring Medina and there will appear to him a man who will be the best or one of the best of the people. He will say 'I testify that you are Ad-Dajjal whose story Allah's Messenger (ﷺ) has told us.' Ad-Dajjal will say (to his audience), 'Look, if I kill this man and then give him life, will you have any doubt about my claim?' They will reply, 'No,' Then Ad-Dajjal will kill that man and then will make him alive. The man will say, 'By Allah, now I recognize you more than ever!' Ad-Dajjal will then try to kill him (again) but he will not be given the power to do so.*"

Source: Sahih al-Bukhari 7132

Narrated Anas bin Malik:

The Prophet (ﷺ) said, "*Ad-Dajjal will come to Medina and find the angels guarding it. So Allah willing, neither Ad-Dajjal, nor plague will be able to come near it.*"

Source: Sahih al-Bukhari 7134

Narrated Abu Bakra:

The Prophet (ﷺ) said, "*The terror caused by Al-Masih Ad-Dajjal will not enter Medina and at that time Medina will have seven gates and there will be two angels at each gate (guarding them).*

Source: Sahih al-Bukhari 7125

In terms of location Medinah since the time of the prophet until today is more virtuous than many places due to the knowledge contained there due to the scholars who live there who inherited knowledge from the prophet. During the trial of the Antichrist, Medina will be physically one of the safest places. So given the fact that we desire safety from the Antichrist we should be preparing for the day when the Antichrist emerges and position ourselves geographically closer and closer to the safe areas like Mecca and Medina. Having the intention will lead to action and such will lead to safety even if we die before the antichrist emerges. Also we must teach our families and descendants to always move ever closer to the safe areas whether it is the area of physical safety from the antichrist or the areas of safety from kufr, shirk and bida. Every generation should move closer to that safe zone so that by the time the trial occurs your descendants will be living in the safe zone. Currently at the time of this writing Permanent Residency is allowed in the Kingdom of Saudi Arabia though expensive it is allowed for non-citizens to live in Mecca or

Medinah permanently until death. So living in Euro-merica as many Muslims do is a risk because when the Antichrist emerges, travel internationally will not be easy to do without compromising one's monotheism. Those who don't live in the Muslim world ahead of time may not even be allowed to leave or enter Muslim territory at such time. Don't wait to migrate until its too late, plan and prepare with sincerity and Allah will make a way. Currently multiple Muslim nations allow citizenship via purchase/investment and others allow permanent residency and renewable residency so options do exist for hijra and it is highly advisable for all and obligatory for most who are able. Every generation should make Hijra closer and closer to the territories of righteousness and safety, nationally, statewide, county to county, neighborhood to neighborhood and house to house ever improving the environment your descendants live in so that they can contribute to the jihad against kufr and the antichrist and against the allies of Iblis. Sadly many are doing reverse-hijra in this era and end up supporting the kuffar militarily via taxes, politically by voting and spiritually by disguising kufr/shirk/bida as Islam. In the end you desire your descendants to be believers from you until the time of the antichrist but living amongst kuffar imperils the bloodline exposing their deen to continuous dilution until it results in apostasy via ignorance and inaction that eventually results in open apostasy after a few generations. So do what you can to move closer to the safe zones and advise your bloodline to always focus on the same hijra oriented goal that leads to paradise.

Abud-Darda' reported:

The Messenger of Allah (ﷺ) said: "*Whoever commits to memory the first ten Ayat of the Surat Al-Kahf, will be protected from (the trial of) Ad-Dajjal (Antichrist).*"

In another narration, the Messenger of Allah (ﷺ) said: "*(Whoever commits to memory) the last ten Ayat of Surat Al-Kahf, he will be protected from (the trial of) Ad-Dajjal (Antichrist).*"

Source: Riyad as-Salihin 1021 Grade: Sahih

It was narrated that Khalid said:

"Humaid narrated: 'Anas - bin Malik - was asked about the torment of the grave and about the Dajjal. He said: "*The Prophet of Allah used to say: Allahumma, inni a'udhu bika minal-kasali, wal-harami, wal-jubni, wal-bukhli, wa fitnatid-dajjali, wa 'adhabil-qabr (O Allah, I seek refuge with You from laziness, old age, cowardice, stinginess, the tribulation of the Dajjal and the torment of the grave.)'"*

Source: Sunan an-Nasa'i 5457 Grade: Hasan

Narrated Abu Huraira:

Allah's Messenger (ﷺ) used to invoke (Allah): *"Allahumma ini a`udhu bika min 'adhabi-l-Qabr, wa min 'adhabi-nnar, wa min fitnati-l-mahya wa-lmamat, wa min fitnati-l-masih ad-dajjal. (O Allah! I seek refuge with you from the punishment in the grave and from the punishment in the Hell fire and from the afflictions of life and death, and the afflictions of Al-Masih Ad-Dajjal."*

Source: Sahih al-Bukhari 1377

Narrated Al-Mughira bin Shu`ba:

Nobody asked the Prophet (ﷺ) as many questions as I asked regarding Ad-Dajjal. The Prophet (ﷺ) said to me, *"What worries you about him?"* I said, "Because the people say that he will have a mountain of bread and a river of water with him (i.e. he will have abundance of food and water)" The Prophet (ﷺ) said, *"Nay, he is too mean to be allowed such a thing by Allah"'* (but it is only to test mankind whether they believe in Allah or in Ad-Dajjal.)

Source: Sahih al-Bukhari 7122

A'isha reported:

I heard the Messenger of Allah (ﷺ) seeking refuge from the trial of Dajjal (Antichrist) in prayer.

Source: Sahih Muslim 587

It was narrated from Aishah that:

the Prophet used to seek refuge with Allah from the torment of the grave and the trial of the Dajjal, and he said: "*You will be tested in your graves.*"

Source: Sunan an-Nasa'i 2065 Grade: Sahih

Narrated Abu Ad-Darda:

that the Prophet (ﷺ) said: "*Whoever recites three Ayat from the beginning of Al-Kahf he is protected from the turmoil of the Dajjal.*"

Source: Jami` at-Tirmidhi 2886 Grade: Sahih

It was narrated that Hudhaifah said:

The Messenger of Allah said: '*I know what the Dajjal will have with him. He will have two flowing rivers, one that appears to the eye to be clear water, and one that appears to the eye to be flaming fire. If anyone sees that, let him go to the river which he thinks is fire and close his eyes, then lower his head and drink from it, for it is cool water. The Dajjal has one blind eye, with a layer of thick skin over it, and between his eyes is written "disbeliever,"* which every believer will read, whether he is literate or illiterate.'

Source: Sahih Muslim 2934b

It was narrated that Hudhaifah said:

"The Messenger of Allah (ﷺ) said: '*The Dajjal (False Christ) is blind in his left eye and has abundant hair. With him will be a Paradise and a Hell, but his Hell is Paradise and his Paradise is Hell.'*"

Source: Sunan Ibn Majah 4071 Grade: Sahih

Uqba bin 'Amr Abu Mas'ud al-Ansari reported:

I went to Hudhaifa bin Yaman and said to him: Narrate what you have heard from Allah's Messenger (ﷺ) pertaining to the Dajjal. *He said that the Dajjal would appear and there would be along with him water and fire and what the people would see as water that would be fire and that would burn and what would appear as fire that would be water and any one of you who would see that should plunge in that which he sees as fire for it would be sweet, pure water,* and 'Uqba said: I also heard it, testifying Hudhaifa.

Source: Sahih Muslim 2935a

Abu Hurairah said:

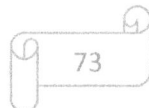

"He (meaning the Prophet) said: '*Seek refuge with Allah from five things: From the torment of Hell, the torment of the grave, the trials of life and death, and the tribulation of Al-Masihid-Dajjal.*'"

Source: Sunan an-Nasa'i 5511 Grade: Sahih

Rib'i bin Hirash said:

I accompanied Abu Mas'ud Al-Ansari to Hudaifah bin Al-Yaman (May Allah be pleased with them). Abu Mas'ud said to him: "Tell us what you heard from the Messenger of Allah (ﷺ) about Dajjal (the Antichrist)." Hudaifah said: He (ﷺ) said, "*Dajjal will appear, and with him will be water and fire. That which people consider to be water will in fact be a burning fire, and that which people will consider to be fire will in fact be cool and sweet water. He who from amongst you happens to face him, should jump into that which he sees as fire for that will be nice and sweet water.*" Abu Mas'ud said: "I have also heard this from the Messenger of Allah (ﷺ)."

Source: Riyad as-Salihin 1809 Grade: Sahih

Abu Huraira reported Allah's Messenger (ﷺ) as saying:

Hasten in performing these good deeds (before these) six things (happen): (the appearance) of the Dajjal, the smoke, the beast of the earth, the rising of the sun from the west, the general turmoil (leading to large-scale massacre) and death of masses and individuals.

Source: Sahih Muslim 2947b

Narrated Abu Huraira:

Allah's Messenger (ﷺ) said, "*Shall I not tell you about the Dajjal a story of which no prophet told his nation? The Dajjal is one-eyed and will bring with him what will resemble Hell and Paradise, and what he will call Paradise will be actually Hell; so I warn you (against him) as Noah warned his nation against him.*"

Source: Sahih al-Bukhari 3338

Az-Zuhri narrated from Salim from Ibn 'Umar who said:

"The Messenger of Allah stood among the people, he praised Allah as is due to Him, then he mentioned the Dajjal and he said: '*Indeed I warn you of him. There has not been a Prophet except that he warned his people, and Nuh indeed warned his people – but I am to say something about him that no Prophet has said to his people: You should know that he is one-eyed, and Allah is certainly not one-eyed.*'" Az-Zuhri said: "'Umar bin Thabit Al-Ansari informed me that some of the Companions of the Prophet informed him, that one day, the Prophet was cautioning them against Fitnah and he said: '*You must know that not one of you will ever see his Lord until he dies. And indeed, he(the Dajjal) has "Kafir" written between his eyes; everyone who is averse to his behavior shall read it.*'"

Source: Jami` at-Tirmidhi 2235 Grade: Sahih

Narrated Ubadah ibn as-Samit:

The Prophet (ﷺ) said: *I have told you so much about the Dajjal (Antichrist) that I am afraid you may not understand. The Antichrist is short, hen-toed, woolly-haired, one-eyed, an eye-sightless, and neither protruding nor deep-seated. If you are confused about him, know that your Lord is not one-eyed.*

Abu Dawud said: 'Amr bin Al-Aswad was appointed a judge.

Source: Sunan Abi Dawud 4320 Grade: Sahih

Narrated `Abdullah bin `Umar:

Allah's Messenger (ﷺ) said, "*Today I saw myself in a dream near the Ka`ba. I saw a whitish brown man, the handsomest of all brown men you might ever see. He had the most beautiful Limma (hair hanging down to the earlobes) you might ever see. He had combed it and it was dripping water; and he was performing the Tawaf around* the Ka`ba leaning on two men or on the shoulders of two men. l asked, "Who is this?" It was said. "Messiah, the son of Mary." Suddenly I saw a curly-haired man, blind in the right eye which looked like a protruding out grape. I asked, "Who is this?" It was said, "He is Masiah Ad-Dajjal."

Source: Sahih al-Bukhari 5902

It was narrated that 'Abdullah bin Mas'ud said:

"On the night on which the Messenger of Allah (ﷺ) was taken on the Night Journey (Isra'), he met Ibrahim, Musa and 'Eisa, and they discussed the Hour. They started with Ibrahim, and asked him about it, but he did not have any knowledge of it. Then they asked Musa, and he did not have any knowledge of it. Then they asked 'Eisa bin Maryam, and he said: 'I have been assigned to some tasks before it happens.' As for as when it will take place, no one knows that except Allah. Then he mentioned Dajjal and said: 'I will descend and kill him, then the people will return to their own lands and will be confronted with Gog and Magog people, who will: "swoop down from every mound."[21:96] They will not pass by any water but they will drink it, (and they will not pass) by anything but they will spoil it. They (the people) will beseech Allah, and I will pray to Allah to kill them. The earth will be filled with their stench and (the people) will beseech

Allah and I will pray to Allah, then the sky will send down rain that will carry them and throw them in the sea. Then the mountains will turn to dust and the earth will be stretched out like a hide. I have been promised that when that happens, the Hour will come upon the people, like a pregnant woman whose family does not know when she will suddenly give birth.'" (One of the narrators) 'Awwam said: "Confirmation of that is found in the Book of Allah, where Allah says: "Until, when Gog and Magog people are let loose (from their barrier), and they swoop down from every mound (21:96)."

Source: Sunan Ibn Majah 4081 Grade: Sahih

Narrated Hudhayfah ibn al-Yaman:

Subay' ibn Khalid said: I came to Kufah at the time when Tustar was conquered. I took some mules from it. When I entered the mosque (of Kufah), I found there some people of moderate stature, and among them was a man whom you could recognize when you saw him that he was from the people of Hijaz.

I asked: Who is he? The people frowned at me and said: Do you not recognize him? This is Hudhayfah ibn al-Yaman, the companion of the Messenger of Allah (ﷺ).

Then Hudhayfah said: People used to ask the Messenger of Allah (ﷺ) about good, and I used to ask him about evil. Then the people stared hard at him.

He said: I know the reason why you dislike it. I then asked: Messenger of Allah, will there be evil as there was before, after this good which Allah has bestowed on us?

He replied: *Yes.* I asked: Wherein does the protection from it lie? He replied: *In the sword.* I asked: Messenger of Allah, what will then happen?

He replied: *If Allah has on Earth a caliph who flays your back and takes your property, obey him, otherwise die holding onto the stump of a tree.*

I asked: What will come next? He replied: *Then the Antichrist (Dajjal) will come forth accompanied by a river and fire. He who falls into his fire will certainly receive his reward, and have his load taken off him, but he who falls into his river will have his load retained and his reward taken off him.*

I then asked: What will come next? He said: *The Last Hour will come.*

Source: Sunan Abi Dawud 4244 Grade Hasan

Abu Huraira reported Allah's Messenger (ﷺ) as saying:

Dajjal will come from the eastern side with the intention of attacking Medina until he will get down behind Uhud. Then the angels will turn his face towards Syria and there he will perish.

Source: Sahih Muslim 1380

Abu Hurairah narrated that the Messenger of Allah said:

"Faith is Yemeni, and disbelief is from the direction of the east. Tranquility is for the people of sheep, and wickedness and Riya is in those who boast among the people of horses and the people of camels. Al-Masih – that is Ad-Dajjal- will come, and when he reaches behind Uhud, the angels will turn his face to the direction of Ash-Sham, and is there that he will be destroyed."

Source: Jami` at-Tirmidhi 2243 Grade: Sahih

Mujammi' bin Jariyah Al-Ansari said:

"I heard the Messenger of Allah saying: *Jesus son of Maryam will kill the Dajjal at the gate of Ludd.'"*

Source: Jami` at-Tirmidhi 2244 Grade: Hasan

An-Nawwas bin Sam`an reported:

One morning the Messenger of Allah (ﷺ) made a mention of Dajjal, and he described him to be insignificant and at the same time described him so significant that we thought he was on the date-palm trees (i.e., nearby). When we went to him (the Prophet (ﷺ)) in the evening, he perceived the sign of fear on our faces. He said, *"What is the matter with you?"* We said: "O Messenger of Allah, you talked about Dajjal this morning raising your voice and lowering it until we thought he was hiding in the palm-trees grove: He said: *"Something other than Dajjal make worry about you. If he appears while I am with you, I will defend you against him. But if he appears after I die, then everyone of you is his own defender. Allah is the One Who remains after me to guide every Muslim. Dajjal will be a young man with very curly hair with one eye protruding (with which he cannot see). I compare (his appearance) to that of Al-`Uzza bin Qatan. He who amongst you survives to see him, should recite over him the opening Ayat of Surat Al-Kahf (i.e., Surat 18: Verses 1-8). He will appear on the way between Syria and Iraq and will spread mischief right and left. O slaves of Allah! Remain adhered to the truth.''* We asked: "O Messenger of Allah! How long will he stay on the earth?" He said, *"For forty days. One day will be like a year, one day like a month, one day like a week and the rest of the days will be like your days.''* We said: "O

Messenger of Allah! Will one day's Salat (prayer) suffice for the Salat of that day which will be equal to one year?" Thereupon he said, "*No, but you must make an estimate of time and then offer Salat.*" We said: "O Messenger of Allah! How quickly will he walk upon the earth?" Thereupon he said, "*Like cloud driven by the wind (i.e., very quickly). He will come to the people and call them to his obedience and they will affirm their faith in him and respond to him. He will then give command to the sky and it will send its rain upon the earth and he will then send his command to the earth and it will grow vegetation. Then in the evening their pasturing animals will come to them with their humps very high and their udders full of milk and their flanks stretched. He will then come to another people and invite them, but they will reject him and he will leave them, in barren lands and without any goods and chattels! He would then walk through the waste land and say to it: `Bring forth your treasures', and the treasures will come out and follow him like swarms of bees. He will then cull a person brimming with youth and strike him with the sword and cut him into two pieces and make these pieces lie at a distance, which is generally between the archer and his target. He will then call that young man and he will come forward, laughing, with his face gleaming out of joy; and it will be at this very time that Allah will send `Isa (Jesus), son of Maryam (Mary) who will descend at* *the white minaret in the eastern side of Damascus, wearing two garments lightly dyed and placing his hands on the wings of two angels. When he will lower his head, there would fall drops of water from his head, and when he will raise it up, drops like pearls would scatter from it. Every disbeliever who will find his (i.e., `Isa's) smell will die and his smell will reach as far as he will be able to see. He will then search for Dajjal until he will catch hold of him at the gate of Ludd (village near Jerusalem), and will kill him. Then the people, whom Allah will have protected, will come to `Isa son of Maryam, and he will wipe their faces and will inform them of their ranks in Jannah, and it will be under such conditions that Allah will reveal to `Isa these words: `I have brought forth from amongst my slaves such people against whom none will be able to fight, so take these people safely to the mountain.' And then Allah will send Ya'juj and Ma'juj (Gog and Magog people) and they will swarm down from every slope. The first of them will pass the Lake Tabariyah (near the Dead Sea in Palestine) and drink all its water. And when the last of them will pass, he will say: `There was once water there.' Prophet `Isa (ﷺ) and his companions will then be so much hard-pressed that the head of an ox will be dearer to them than one hundred dinar, and `Isa along with his companions, will make supplication to Allah, Who will send insects which will attack their (Ya'juj and Ma'juj people) neck until they all* *will perish like a single person. Prophet, Isa and his companions will then come down and they will not find in the earth as much space as a single span which would not be filled with their corpses and their stench. Prophet `Isa and his companions will then again beseech Allah, Who will send birds whose necks will be like those of Bactrian camels, and they will carry them and throw them where Allah will desire. Then Allah will send down rain which will spare no house in the city or in the countryside. It would wash away the earth until it appears like a mirror. Then the earth will be told to bring forth its fruit and restore its blessings; and as a result of this, there will grow such a big pomegranate that a group of people will eat from it and seek shelter under its skin. Milk will be so blessed that the milk of one she-camel will suffice for a large company and the cow will give so much milk, that it will suffice for a whole tribe. The sheep will give so much milk that the whole family will be able to drink out of that, and at that time Allah will send a pleasant wind which will soothe people even under their armpits, and will take the life of every Muslim and true believer, and only the wicked will survive. They will commit adultery in public like asses and the Resurrection Day will be held.''*

Source: Riyad as-Salihin 1808 Grade: Sahih

Abu Huraira reported Allah's Messenger (ﷺ) as saying:

The Last Hour would not come until the Romans would land at al-A'maq or in Dabiq. An army consisting of the best (soldiers) of the people of the earth at that time will come from Medina (to counteract them). When they will arrange themselves in ranks, the Romans would say: Do not stand between us and those (Muslims) who took prisoners from amongst us. Let us fight with them; and the Muslims would say: Nay, by Allah, we would never get aside from you and from our brethren that you may fight them. They will then fight and a third (part) of the army would run away, whom Allah will never forgive. A third (part of the army) which would be constituted of excellent martyrs in Allah's eye, would be killed and the third who would never be put to trial would win and they would be conquerors of Constantinople. And as they would be busy in distributing the spoils of war (amongst themselves) after hanging their swords by the olive trees, the Satan would cry: The Dajjal has taken your place among your family. They would then come out, but it would be of no avail. And when they would come to Syria, he would come out while they would be still preparing themselves for battle drawing up the ranks. Certainly, the time of prayer shall come and then Jesus (peace be upon him) son of Mary would descend and would lead them. When the enemy of Allah would see him, it would (disappear) just as the salt dissolves itself in water and if he (Jesus) were not to confront them at all, even then it would dissolve completely, but Allah would kill them by his hand and he would show them their blood on his lance (the lance of Jesus Christ).

Source: Sahih Muslim 2897

It was narrated from An-Nawwas bin Sam'an, who said:

"The Messenger of Allah mentioned the Dajjal one morning, he belittled him and mentioned his importance until we thought that he might be amidst a cluster of date-palms." He said: "We departed from the presence of the Messenger of Allah, then we returned to him, and he noticed that(concern) in us. *So he said: 'What is wrong with you?'*" We said: 'O Messenger of Allah! You mentioned the Dajjal this morning, belittling him, and mentioning his importance until we thought that he might be amidst a cluster of the date-palms.' *He said: 'It is not the Dajjal that I fear for you. If he were to appear while I am among you, then I will be his adversary on your behalf. And if he appears and I am not among you, then each man will have to fend for himself. And Allah will take care of every Muslim after me. He is young, with curly hair, his eyes protruding, resembling someone from 'Abdul-Uzza bin Qatan. Whoever among you sees him, then let him recite the beginning of Surah Ashab Al-Kahf.'" He said: 'He will appear from what is between Ash-Sham and Al-'Iraq, causing devastation toward the right and toward the left. O worshippers of Allah! Hold fast!'" We said: 'O Messenger of Allah! How long will he linger on the earth?' He said: 'Forty days, a day like a year, a day like a month, a day like a week, and the remainder of his days are like your days.'" We said: 'O Messenger of Allah! Do you think that during the day that is like a year, the Salat of one day will be sufficient for us?' He said: 'No. You will have to estimate it.' We said: 'O Messenger of Allah! How fast will he move through the earth.' He said: 'Like a rain storm driven by the wind. He will come upon a people and call them, and they will deny him, and reject his claims. Then he will leave them, and their wealth will follow him. They will awaken in the morning with nothing left. Then he will come upon a people and call them, and they will respond to him, believing in him. So he will order the Heavens to bring rain, and it shall rain, and he will order the land to sprout, and it will sprout. Their cattle will return to them with their coats the longest, their udders the fullest and their stomachs the fattest.' He said: 'Then he will come upon some ruins, saying to it: "Bring me your treasures!" He will turn to leave it, and it will follow him, like drone bees. Then he will call a young man, full of youth, and he will strike him with the sword cutting him into two pieces. Then he will call him, and he will come forward with his face beaming and laughing. So while he is doing that, 'Eisa bin Mariam, peace be upon him, will descend in eastern Damascus at the white minaret, between two Mahrud, with his hands on the wings of two angels. When he lowers his head, drops fall, and when raises it, gems like pearls drop from him.' He said: 'His breath does not reach anyone but he dies, and his breath reaches as far as his sight.' He said: 'So he pursues him(the Dajjal) and he catches up with him at the gate of Ludd where he kills him.' He said: 'So he remains there as long as Allah wills.' He said: 'Then Allah reveals to him: "Take my slaves to At-Tur, for I have sent down some creatures of Mine which no one shall be able to kill.'" He said: 'Allah dispatches Ya'juj and Ma'juj, and they are as Allah said: They swoop down from every mount.' "He said: 'The first of them pass by the lake of Tiberias, drinking what is in it. Then the last of them pass by it saying: "There was water here at one time." They travel until they reach a mountain at Bait Al-Maqdis. They will say: "We have killed whoever was in the earth. Come! Let us kill whoever is in the skies." They will shoot their arrows into the Heavens, so Allah will return their arrows to them red with blood. Eisa bin Mariam and his Companions be surrounded, until the head of a bull on that day would be better to them than a hundred Dinar to one of you today.'*

"He said: "Eisa will beseech Allah, as will his companions.' He said: 'So Allah will send An-Naghaf down upon their necks. In the morning they will find that they have all died like the death of a single soul.' He said: " 'Eisa and his companions will come down, and no spot nor hand-span can be found, except that it is filled with their stench, decay and blood. So 'Eisa will beseech Allah, as will his companions.' So Allah will send upon them birds like the necks of Bukht(milch)camels.' They will carry them off and cast them into an abyss. The Muslims will burn their bows, arrows and quivers for seventy years.' "He said: 'Allah will send upon them a rain which no house of hide nor mud will bear. The earth will be washed, leaving it like a mirror. Then it will be said to the earth: "bring forth your fruits and return your blessings." So on that day, a whole troop would eat a pomegranate and seek shade under its skin. Milk will be so blessed that a large group of people will be sufficed by one milking of a camel. And that a tribe will be sufficed by one milking of a cow, and that a group will be sufficed by the milking of sheep. While it is like that, Allah will send a wind which grabs the soul of every believer, leaving the remainder of the people copulating publicly like the copulation of donkeys. Upon them the Hour shall begin.' "

Source: Jami` at-Tirmidhi 2240 Grade: Sahih

Abdullah bin 'Amr bin Al-said:

The Messenger of Allah (ﷺ) said, "*Dajjal (the Antichrist) will appear in my Ummah and he will stay in the world for forty. I do not know whether this will be forty days or forty months or forty years. Allah will then send (Prophet) 'Isa (Jesus), son of Maryam (Mary). 'Isa will pursue him and slaughter him. Then people will survive for seven years (i.e., after the demise of 'Isa) in the state that there will be no rancour between two persons. Then Allah will send a cool breeze from the side of Ash-Sham. None will remain upon the face of the earth having the smallest particle of good or Faith in him but he will die, so much so that even if someone amongst you will enter the innermost part of a mountain, this breeze will reach that place also and will cause him to die. Only the wicked people will survive and they will be as fast as birds (i.e., to commit evil) and as ferocious towards one another as wild beasts. They will never appreciate the good, nor condemn evil. Then Shaitan (Satan) will come to them in the garb of a man and will say: 'Will you not obey me?' They will say: 'What do you order us to do?' He will command them to worship idols. They will have abundance of sustenance and will lead comfortable lives. Then the Trumpet will be blown. Every one hearing it, will turn his neck towards it and will raise it. The first one to hear that Trumpet will be a man who will be busy repairing the basin for his camels. He will become unconscious. Allah will send, or will cause to send, rain which will be like dew and there will grow out of it (like wild growth) the bodies of the people. Then the second Trumpet will be blown and they will stand up and begin to look around. Then it will be said: 'O people! Go to your Lord.' Then there will be a command: 'Make them stand there.' After it they will be called to account. Then it will be said: 'Separate from them the share of the Fire.' It will be asked: 'How much?' It will be said: 'Nine hundred and ninety-nine out of every thousand.' That will be the Day which will make children hoary-headed men because of its terror and that will be the Day when the Shin will be uncovered."*

Source: Riyad as-Salihin 1810 Grade: Sahih

It was narrated that Thawban, the freed slave of the Messenger of Allah (ﷺ), said:

"The Messenger of Allah (ﷺ) said: *'There are two groups of my Ummah whom Allah will free from the Fire: The group that invades India, and the group that will be with 'Isa bin Maryam, peace be upon him.'*"

Source: Sunan an-Nasa'i 3175 Grade: Hasan

Narrated Abu Huraira:

Allah's Messenger (ﷺ) said, "*By Him in Whose Hands my soul is, surely (Jesus,) the son of Mary will soon descend amongst you and will judge mankind justly (as a Just Ruler); he will break the Cross and kill the pigs and there will be no Jizya (i.e. taxation taken from non-Muslims). Money will be in abundance so that nobody will accept it, and a single prostration to Allah (in prayer) will be better than the whole world and whatever is in it.*" Abu Huraira added "If you wish, you can recite (this verse of the Book): -- 'And there is none Of the people of the Scriptures (Jews and Christians) But must believe in him (i.e Jesus as an Apostle of Allah and a human being) Before his death. And on the Day of Judgment He will be a witness Against them." (4.159)

Source: Sahih al-Bukhari 3448

Narrated Abu Hurayrah:

The Prophet (ﷺ) said: *There is no prophet between me and him, that is, Jesus (﷿). He will descent (to the earth). When you see him, recognise him: a man of medium height, reddish fair, wearing two light yellow garments, looking as if drops were falling down from his head though it will not be wet. He will fight the people for the cause of Islam. He will break the cross, kill swine, and abolish jizyah. Allah will perish all religions except Islam. He will destroy the Antichrist and will live on the earth for forty years and then he will die. The Muslims will pray over him.*

Source: Sunan Abi Dawud 4324 Grade: Sahih

Narrated `Aisha:

The Prophet (ﷺ) used to say, "*O Allah! I seek refuge with You from laziness from geriatric old age, from being in debt, and from committing sins. O Allah! I seek refuge with You from the punishment of the Fire, the afflictions of the grave, the punishment in the grave, and the evil of the affliction of poverty and from the evil of the affliction caused by Al-Masih Ad-Dajjal. O Allah! Wash away my sins with the water of snow and hail, and cleanse my heart from the sins as a white garment is cleansed of filth, and let there be a far away distance between me and my sins as You have set far away the East and the West from each other.*"

Source: Sahih al-Bukhari 6375

Abu Hurairah reported:

Messenger of Allah (ﷺ) said, "*Hasten to do good deeds before you are overtaken by one of the seven afflictions.*" Then (giving a warning) he said, "*Are you waiting for such poverty which will make you unmindful of devotion; or prosperity which will make you corrupt, or disease as will disable you, or such senility as will make you mentally unstable, or sudden death, or Ad-Dajjal who is the worst expected absent, or the Hour, and the Hour will be most grievous and most bitter*".

Source: Riyad as-Salihin 93 Grade: Hasan

Urwah bin Az-Zubair (narrated) that he heard Asma' bint Abi Bakr say:

"The Messenger of Allah stood up and mentioned the trial with which a person will be tested in his grave. When he mentioned that the people became restless, which prevented me from understanding what the Messenger of Allah had said. When they settled down, I said to a man who was near me: 'May Allah bless you, what did the end?' he said: '*It has been revealed to me that you will be tested in your graves with a trial close to that of the Dajjal.*'"

Source: Sunan an-Nasa'i 2062 Grade: Sahih

It was narrated that Abu Sa'eed said:

"The Messenger of Allah (ﷺ) came out to us when we were discussing Dajjal (False Christ) and said: '*Shall I not tell you of that which I fear more for you than Dajjal?*' We said: 'Yes.' He said: '*Hidden polytheism, when a man stands to pray and makes it look good because he sees a man looking at him.*'"

Source: Sunan Ibn Majah 4204 Grade: Hasan